Making Content Work

Tips, tools and templates for your brand or business

Contents

Introduction

It's no secret that 'content is king'. With the growth of ecommerce and all things digital, brands and businesses are playing in a whole new arena: online. This shift into a digital era brought with it a new media landscape too, and along came blogs, quick access to video (hello, YouTube), competing for top spots in Google, and of course, social media.

Our consumption of content - whether that's an online article, a Twitter thread, images or video - is showing no signs of slowing down. And any brand or business that wants to compete should be making content a key focus for their brand building and marketing efforts.

But... It can be easier said than done. From small brands to big, content is often a head scratcher. Throughout my career, I've come up against the same questions time and again from business owners, marketing teams, and CEOs...

How do we create a content strategy?
What content should we produce?
How do we create content?
How do we grow our Instagram/TikTok following?
Should we work with influencers? How do we do that?
How does 'content' translate to sales?

This book is here to navigate the minefield of content, specifically in the online space. It's aimed at small brands because in my experience, they're less likely to have the teams, budgets, and human power to focus loads of time on their content efforts. But it would work just as well for big brands too.

I'll demystify content, and give you tools and templates to help you get the best out of your time (and money). So grab a pen and a fresh pad of paper, and get ready to make some notes.

Why Me

Chances are if you're reading this, then you've probably already spent hours reading articles or speaking with experts about content. Where I differ, is that I do this every day and have done throughout my career.

I've spent more than 10 years in content roles in some form or another. I've worked in journalism, writing news stories and features in a small team of two. I've led the fashion and lifestyle content marketing team at a large UK-based ecommerce group. I've spent time at a content agency specialising in creating content for businesses within the interior design and architecture sector. And I've been the global content lead at an international skincare company.

I'm now freelance, working with a mix of big global brands and agencies, and small brands that are just starting out. On the side, I run my own Instagram account where I showcase my personal style and regularly collaborate with brands to share their products with my audience of more than 32,000 followers.

Every day, I'm creating content, testing content, adapting to new platforms and consumer behaviours, and seeing which brands are smashing it with their content.

Chapter 1

Defining Your Brand

Before you start diving into any content-related activity, it's important to understand **what and who your brand is**. This is the starting point and a good reference point for any kind of activity you do, whether it's sales, promotions, how you talk about certain holidays and occasions throughout the year, and partnerships with other brands or influencers.

Consistency is key for building brand recognition and when it comes to the creation process, it helps you and the people creating content for you, keep it 'on brand'. Without this in place, your content and how you present your brand can soon become messy and give a confusing message to your audience.

Think about what you are as a brand (and what you're not). Consider your brand personality - if you were a person, what would you be like? What would your interests be? Where would you travel, shop, spend your free time?

Consider any brand adjacencies and where you sit in the market. Are you luxury or mass market? Do you, as a brand, have any values you want to get across? What do you want to sound like when you write?

If you're struggling to nail who you are as a brand, consider the following questions as prompts and create a document that can be used by you and your team.

Product / Service

- What products do you offer?
- What will the products do?
- Who is your target market?
- Where will these products sit in the market?
- What are similar / reference products in the market?
- What are your key marketing claims?
- What problem are you solving with these products?

Brand

- What's your point of difference?
- Who are your competitors?
- Are there any other brands you'd like to align with?
- How would you describe the personality of the brand? If the brand was a person, what would it be like?
- What's your customer profile? (i.e., age, gender, location, interests, where they shop and what their hobbies are, what social platforms they use)
- What's your brand manifesto / elevator pitch?
- What are your core brand values?

Tone of Voice

- How do you want to sound? Are you funny, cheeky, rebellious? Or are you formal, serious, matter of fact?
- What vocabulary do you use?
- What vocabulary do you not use?
- Are you a stickler for grammar or do you speak in a more conversational manner?
- Do you use sensory, descriptive language or are you more of a 'less is more' brand?
- How do you want your audience to feel when they read your copy?

When you consider brand adjacencies, take a look at how they present themselves and use these questions to come up with a review of what they're doing. This can help you see other brands' approaches, and you can quickly see who you want to sound/present like and who you don't.

Once you have this in place, you'll also want to establish some visual guidelines. Do you have certain brand colours and fonts? What's your photography and video style like?

Chapter 2

What Is Content?

I can't tell you how many times I've sat in a meeting or a boardroom and been told "we don't have enough content" or "we need more content". And when I ask what kind of content they need more of, I'm met with a blank face. 'Content' has become such a buzzword that it's almost lost meaning.

The truth is, 'content' is an **umbrella term**. There are loads of different types and depending on what your business is and who your audience is, you may want to lean on one or a few types.

1. Blogs

Blogging exploded onto the scene in the early-mid 2000s (fashion blog readers will remember the heyday when Tavi Gevinson's Style Rookie and Chiara Ferragni's The Blonde Salad were the go-to for all things style).

Brands soon started to take note too. Net-A-Porter published editorial content relevant to their product offering and audience, and any brand worth their salt was offering an SEO-driven blog that would not only cement them as industry expert leaders but would give them coveted Google real estate.

According to The State of Content Marketing Report 2019: Global Report, blogs account for 86 per cent of content marketing. They provide valuable insight for the user, can be useful for explaining tricky concepts or go deeper into a product, and can help drive valuable traffic to your website.

2. Video

We've all seen the rise of YouTube and more recently, TikTok. Many consumers now expect video to be part of a brand experience, whether it's a styling reel for a new item of clothing on Instagram or an informative 'how to' of assembling a piece of furniture on a website's product page.

3. Social media posts

There are billions of social media users worldwide and social media has reached a point where it's infiltrated almost every part of our lives. Interiors are styled to be 'Instagrammable', little-known brands can find overnight fame thanks to TikTok, and YouTube is our go-to for tutorials on just about anything.

Not every social media platform will be relevant for your brand or business though, so identify which platforms your audience is using and create content that will speak to them.

Social media is also a great place to network. Build relationships with your customers and influencers to help your content reach further - and get first-hand insight into what content your audience connects with.

4. User-generated content

Or 'UGC'. This falls mainly into the social media category but is a content type all its own. An example of UGC is an Instagram user taking an image of your product and posting it to their account.

With their permission, you can reuse that image on your own marketing channels. It gives your brand and product social proof (i.e., it shows your target audience that other people use and enjoy your product) and gives you content without you having to create it.

5. Reviews and testimonials

Word of mouth is a powerful marketing tool. Think about the number of times you've gone to a restaurant because a friend recommended it or chosen a new fitness class because a colleague waxed lyrical about it.

In the digital age, online reviews and testimonials are an extension of that. Real people leaving real thoughts on your product or service can be highly valuable for persuading a shopper to purchase. Reviews can also be repurposed into social media posts and used in emails.

6. Infographics

Infographics are a simple yet effective and engaging way of getting key elements of information across. It could be statistics about your sustainability efforts, or a timeline that showcases the history of your heritage brand. Infographics can be used in blog posts, web pages, and social media platforms such as LinkedIn, Pinterest, Facebook, Instagram, and Twitter. A great thing about infographics is that they're also highly shareable (so make you include your branding somewhere, so people know you're the original source).

7. Podcasts

Once dominated by true crime fans, there are now thousands of podcasts on every topic going. A branded podcast that provides quality content for your target audience is a great way to build brand awareness and establish yourself as an industry leader.

The best branded podcasts provide valuable, original content - they're not there to be outright advertising for your product or service. Take Penguin Random House's podcast, for example. They interview authors in their fortnightly podcast, offering their listeners 'insider' content they know they'll be interested in, without overtly pushing their audience to buy their books.

8. Emails

Email marketing is a huge business. It allows you to reach a targeted audience who have already signed up to hear what you have to say, and you can measure exactly what your database is engaging with - and what they're not.

Email marketing can come in the form of newsletters, product, or collection launches, or offers such as seasonal sales. Emails are also a powerful tool for driving traffic to your other content, such as your blog posts, podcast, or webinar.

9. eBooks and White Papers

Long-form content that provides value to your audience can be hugely beneficial to your business. eBooks and white papers are often 'gated' content, too, which means to access them, users will have to sign up to your email database, giving you a valuable lead.

eBooks go into depth about a certain topic, making them useful tools if you'd like to establish yourself or your brand as a thought leader. White papers, on the other hand, are more like research papers, filled with stats and data that provide insight.

Publishing original research on a topical subject is likely to be shared by media and influencers, giving your content more reach. Highsnobiety does white papers well, doing deep dives on subjects that are relevant to their audience, such as luxury fashion and gamification.

10. Webinars

Webinars are online events, seminars, training events or presentations delivered to a select audience. They're often used by education or CPD (continuing professional development) providers but can also be used by brands to host 'exclusive' question and answer sessions with a brand ambassador, deliver tutorials or host a panel discussion.

You'll benefit from email sign ups, and by limiting attendees to a certain number, you'll also generate excitement and demand.

11. Interactive content

Interactive content such as quizzes are a fun way for your audience to engage in your brand or product. Let's say you have a haircare brand and you've just launched different ranges for different hair types. Your quiz could be geared towards asking the users questions about their hair, their scalp, and what they're looking for in a product, with the end result recommending the product that is best suited to them. By sending the results via email, you could also capture more email addresses for your database.

Chapter 3

How To Choose Your Content Types

Not all content types will be relevant to your brand - and you probably won't have the capacity to create all either. In fact, you'll probably benefit from focusing on a few types of content and then using what you create in the most efficient way, so you get the most out of it that you possibly can.

This all comes down to your **business goals and your audience**. If you're a B2B business offering educational content, your audience will benefit from webinars, eBooks, and white papers (and you'll generate more leads as this content is often gated). Your audience will likely spend their social media time on LinkedIn, so that's where you should show up too.

If you're a skincare brand, your audience will benefit from educational 'how to' videos that detail the steps in a skincare routine or show how much to use of each product. They'll also read blogs that go into the science of a new product, or that give advice on what product to use if their skin is dry or sensitive, for example.

Always think about who your target audience is and where they spend their time. Are they on TikTok? Instagram? Twitter? What content are they sharing? How do they talk about the topics or products they're sharing? Keeping them and their behaviours in mind will help keep your content efforts focused.

Always think about purpose too. What are you trying to achieve with your content? What are you hoping your audience will take away from it when they see it or interact with it? If you want to drive traffic to your website, are you doing it effectively? If you want to create shareable content for social media, is it original, entertaining, or informative enough?

Establish your goals before you start creating. It will help you stay focused and prevent you from spending lots of time (and money) creating things that won't give you your desired effect.

Chapter 4

Coming Up With Ideas

One of the biggest challenges when it comes to content is the idea phase. It's the sweet spot between being creative and strategic - but once you've covered your initial ideas, it can be difficult to know what to do next. You also want to make sure you're original, on-brand and consistent to build brand authority while adapting to changes in culture, trends, new platforms… and everything else that's going on in the world.

Content pillars

To keep on track (and to prevent falling into the trap of simply copying your competitors), create 4-5 content pillars and break each pillar down into different ways of executing that pillar.

Think of your content pillars as what makes your brand unique. Does your founder have an inspirational story? Are your products highly innovative with lots of opportunity to deep dive into the making of them? Maybe you're a fashion brand that creates clothing with only recycled materials, so you have a strong stance on sustainability and ethical production? Or maybe you're a restaurant that only uses organic, seasonal ingredients? These can all start to form your content pillars.

The following two content pillars are a couple I came up with for an online jewellery retailer.

Pillar 1: Our Brands

- Share new collections and why specific pieces were chosen
- Tell the stories of jewellery designers
- Share insider info on the inspiration behind designing collections
- Go behind the scenes of jewellery workshops to show the creative process

Pillar 2: Pearls of Wisdom

- Spotlight the latest jewellery trends and how to wear them
- Educate with guides and tips for what to consider when buying jewellery: e.g. How to find your ring size
- Share styling tips: e.g. How to mix metals, how to stack your rings
- Show the best ways to care for jewellery

Once you have your pillars in place and documented, it all starts to become easier. When you're planning out your content for the month (or quarter, or year), you can refer to your content pillars and start to build out your ideas and campaigns from there. In chapter 8, I'll give you a template for creating a content calendar to keep all that planning in one place.

Listen to your audience

Publishing content in the online sphere can be both a blessing and a curse. We have direct access to our audience - and our audience has direct access to our business or brand. On the negative end of the scale, this can bring about customer complaints in very open spaces, trolling, or 'cancelling' of brands.

But on the positive end of the scale, being able to speak directly with our audience not only helps build brand relationships, it gives us direct insight into their pain points, their likes, and their dislikes.

Take a close look at the kind of content **they're sharing**. What are they talking about? How are they engaging with others on their own social platforms?

And take a close look at **how they're speaking with you**. What comments are they leaving on your social media posts? What questions are they asking in your DMs (direct messages)? Outside of social media, speak with your customer service team. What questions are your customers asking? These can all help you come up with ideas for what content to address next - and show your customers you're listening.

Trends

In the digital landscape, trends move very quickly. A topic can be 'hot' for a few days before people move on, and on social media, there always seems to be a new trending video format or Twitter meme.

When it comes to trends, I'd say tread carefully. Firstly, it's impossible to jump on every trend because they move so quickly.

Secondly, it's important to consider your brand. Not every trend will be right for you and there have been numerous times that I've seen brands do something for a few likes, but it just doesn't sit right with their ethos or their core audience.

When you spot trends in digital content, always think: **"is it right for our brand?"**

If you're unsure, refer to your brand guidelines or your content pillars. If it doesn't align, avoid it - it could end up doing more harm to your brand than good.

Review your competitors (and beyond)

It's always a good idea to keep an eye on your competitors. Not to copy, but to see what they're doing - and what they're not doing. What gaps can you fill? How can you differentiate your brand and product offering through your content?

Take a look at other 'successful' brands outside your industry too. How are they using content to build brand awareness, or talk about their product or service? **Looking outside your niche can help spark inspiration** and think differently from your competitors.

Look at media titles too. Newspapers, magazines, online editorial sites. Are there certain topics they push more than most? Do they have a clear and engaging way of presenting complex inspiration through images, graphs or infographics?

When you carry out these reviews, put your findings in an 'inspiration' folder that you can refer to again and again.

Chapter 5

One Idea = Multiple Content Types

One of the most effective ways of using content is to take one idea and turn it into **multiple pieces of content**. That way one idea can effectively cover a couple of weeks' marketing activity, without you straining to come up with multiple ideas. It also helps you get a message across in multiple ways, reaching your audience through different platforms and mediums.

Let's say you're a natural skincare brand and you're launching a new serum. The results from your clinical trials show it can help increase collagen production in skin, thanks to a plant extract you've used. This is a big selling point in a competitive market and reiterates one of the reasons you'll always favour natural ingredients.

Here's how that could be turned into multiple pieces of content:

1. An infographic showcasing the stats and the science, shared on social media
2. A blog post explaining the science behind the product and the importance of collagen production for skin, featuring quotes from your product development team and subject matter experts
3. Sharing customer reviews that reflect this increase in collagen, in emails and on social media

4. Before and after images of customers or influencers who have used the product for a certain period of time, visibly showing plumper skin or a reduction in fine lines

5. Videos from relevant influencers, showcasing them using the product and giving their honest opinion. These videos can be shared on YouTube, TikTok, Instagram, Facebook, and your website

With this, we're essentially talking about the same thing, but we're taking a slightly different angle or approach depending on the content type and giving you lots of content to play with.

Chapter 6

How To Produce Content

Now it's time to actually create the content, which for lots of brands who don't have an in-house content team or production studio, can feel pretty daunting. Small brands, especially, don't always have the budgets, the time or the skill sets needed to create everything they want to create but the good thing is, there are loads of people out there who do.

For the instance of this book, I'll focus on **outsourcing content**, which can be a cost-effective way of getting everything you need. You get quality content when you need it, without having to hire permanent staff, which may not be possible (or necessary) for some brands.

When you outsource content, the experts create the content, then deliver the work to you to do as you wish. Make sure you have agreements around image/video rights and usage in place ahead of each project and in writing, so you're completely covered when it comes to using the content they've created for you.

Working with freelancers

A big bulk of my work as a freelancer is copywriting. Brands engage me to write copy for seasonal campaigns across their website, email, blog and social media - or if they're just starting out, they might ask me to create a tone of voice for them and write all the copy for their website.

It's not just copywriting that you can outsource. There are brand strategists if you want help really defining your brand, photographers, videographers, and graphic designers who can design your logo or website and create email templates.

It can take a bit of work to find the right fit (ask your network for recommendations, scour LinkedIn, or look on creative job/networking sites like The Dots) but once you do, you could end up with good, long-term relationships with experts that you can lean on whenever you need them.

Working with influencers

If your focus is content for social media, working with influencers can be a smart way to have new content created that you can use, and tapping into an already-established audience.

Find influencers within your niche who have a **good following and solid engagement** (i.e., the number of likes and comments in relation to their following. An account with 10,000 followers that's averaging 2,000 likes and 25 genuine comments per post is much more likely to have an authentic, engaged audience than an account with 70,000 followers that's averaging 1,000 likes and 5 comments per post.).

This can take a bit of leg work in the beginning. You can find influencers by searching hashtags that are relevant to your brand or product offering or going onto competitor brands' accounts and see who they're featuring - or look in their tagged images to see who's featuring them. If you're looking for location-specific influencers, you can search that location too, and see who pops up.

One thing I'd recommend when it comes to working with influencers, is not to work with only one 'type' that checks the same boxes. Keep it on brand, yes, but make sure you're diversifying enough so you're **reaching different audiences**. Work with different age groups, different countries (if your product is available in more than one), different genders and different account focuses.

A brand selling glass and dinnerware, for example, could work with an influencer that creates recipes and shares them on their account, an influencer that focuses on interior styling, and a fashion influencer that's just about to move into a new home. They all make sense to team up with your brand but they're different enough that you'll be able to tap into different audiences.

You can then send those influencers your product in exchange for a post on their account and the rights for you to use their image/video. Some influencers will ask for payment, while some will be happy with just the product. You could also offer them a discount code and commission for any sales attributed to their post, as part of your negotiations.

Working with content creators

Content creators, for me, are almost a mix of freelancers and influencers. They tend to be amateur photographers or videographers who create beautiful content and post it to their social media channels.

They may not have loads of followers (like influencers do), but I've had a lot of success working with content creators for social media specifically, and it tends to be a very cost-effective way of getting a bank of images or video that you can use again and again. They know how the platforms work, so they know how to create content that will suit.

You might come across an Instagram account with 4,000 followers (low in influencer standards) but their photography is incredible. You won't get much from them if working with them on an influencer basis (i.e., they don't have a large audience you can tap into), but you could engage them to take a series of photographs of your product that you can then use.

They'll need payment as you'll be buying the rights for their content to be used across your marketing channels, which can all be ironed out in the negotiation process. Like finding influencers, this can take a bit of trawling through the social platforms you want to create content for, but once you have your list of go-to creators, you can continue to work with them on a regular basis.

The briefing process

When you're outsourcing content production, it's really important to **get your brief right**. I've worked at or with brands who engage a freelancer or influencer to create a piece of content, only to be really disappointed with what they get back. But if you looked at the brief, it's quite often unsurprising that some things go amiss.

You or your team may know everything there is to know about your brand, what style you like or what it is you're trying to achieve with your content but the person you're engaging won't. So be detailed, even if it feels like you're going overboard.

Here's what you should include:

- An overview of the project and the task in hand
- Deadlines
- Exact deliverables with formats and how to supply them (e.g., 1 x blog post in a Word document, 3 x portrait images, 1 x 30 second video in portrait mode)
- Tone of voice guidelines (for writers)
- Brand guidelines
- Mood boards or links to inspiration
- Any 'must haves' (e.g., the blog post must include certain keywords and links, or there must be one image that shows a certain detail of a product)

Chapter 7

Create, Then Distribute (And Repurpose)

You've got your ideas and you've created your content, now it's time to share (or 'distribute') it. After all, it's no use spending all that time creating exceptional content if you're not going to let people see it.

This is where your planning and strategy head comes in. How are you going to make the most of your content? How are you going to achieve your goal, whether that be growing your email list, increasing your social media followers or driving more traffic to certain pages on your website?

It all goes back to what I mentioned in chapter 3: purpose. Knowing why you're creating your content helps you create it and knowing what you want it to achieve helps you plan how you use it.

Distributing your content

Let's say you own, or work for, a flooring business. You sell different types of wood and vinyl flooring that can be configured in different ways to create different patterns, so you've created a video that shows all the different ways you can use the flooring, giving lots of valuable inspiration and know-how for your potential customers.

Why? Because you've discovered, through conversations with your customer service team or sales team, that most of your potential customers don't realise just how versatile it is and as a result, you're probably losing out on sales.

You could be forgiven for uploading that video to YouTube and hoping for the best, but that probably won't give you your desired outcome (i.e., more traffic to your website and more sales).

Here are some other ways you could use that video:

- Post it on your relevant product pages, so when customers visit your website, they can see how they can use these different types of flooring
- Create edited cuts of the video that can be posted to your Instagram, TikTok, and Facebook feeds
- Share those videos in your Instagram and Facebook Stories, with a link going directly to the relevant product pages
- Write an inspirational 'get the look' blog post, embedding the video into the post
- Share a link to that blog post in an email

Repurposing your content

I've seen a lot of teams and brands pushing themselves to the limit to create loads of content. And I've sat in countless meetings where departments and senior members of a company simply demand 'more content'. Yes, creating new content keeps things fresh and exciting but simply focusing on 'more, more, more' can lead to burn out and creating new content purely for the sake of having new content.

Instead, dedicate time each month or quarter to **look back on what you've already done**. Do you have a blog post that you wrote a year ago that still gets loads of traffic and backlinks? Keep it updated with relevant information and fresh links and if it makes sense to do so, turn aspects of that blog post into a video for your social channels or use it to create an email. The appetite amongst your audience is clearly there, so make the most of it.

Or are there certain pins on Pinterest that got loads of saves? Pin it again. Those images on Instagram that got saved and shared more than most? Post it again, after a bit of time has passed and your followers have probably forgotten about it.

Better yet, use those social posts to spark inspiration for more content. What were people saying in the comments? What did they like about it? Take those learnings to inform more content. If they were asking questions or for more information, host a Q&A session or write a blog post that goes into more detail.

In chapter 9, I'll go into more detail about what metrics to measure for each channel, and how you can summarise your findings to inform future ideas.

Chapter 8

The Content Calendar

I'm a big fan of planning. It keeps teams focussed, ensures you're always thinking strategically, and prevents spending hours of your day trying to think of what to do.

With digital content, it's important to be flexible. Sometimes things happen and you need to adapt. Something might happen in the world - like, say, a global pandemic - and suddenly the content you've planned isn't relevant or appropriate, so always have your wits about you. But having that plan in place helps you quickly spot where you might need to change something and stops that panic from setting in when you do.

Enter the content calendar: A documented plan of what you're doing on what channel and when. This can be shared amongst your team so everyone knows what's going on and will know to expect a spike in sales of a certain product if you're pushing it, or an increase in traffic to certain pages on your website.

Some people like to incorporate their content calendar into their marketing calendar, some like to create a separate one that purely focuses on content. For the sake of this book, I'll focus purely on a separate monthly content calendar.

Here's what to include:

- Key seasonal dates (e.g., holidays such as Valentine's Day or Mother's Day, if they're relevant to your brand)
- Key brand dates (e.g., a new product or collection launch)
- Content focus per channel

The following table is how I set up a content calendar, with fictionalised examples and dates. This looks at a week, but you could keep it going for as long as you'd like.

At the top of the calendar, I lay the week out day by day, followed by any key dates underneath (note: some weeks there won't be any 'key' dates, which is fine. You actually don't want too many key dates, or you'll end up trying to focus on too many things).

Underneath that, I include a row for laying out what content pillar it falls under. This helps you make sure you're not deviating from your pillars and helps you see if you're focusing too much on one or two pillars, or if there's a relatively even split.

I then break it down per channel, with a description of what's happening on that channel each day. Your channels may look different to this, depending on which ones you're focusing on or using.

The Content Calendar

	Monday 01/02/23	Tuesday 02/02/23	Wednesday 03/02/23	Thursday 04/02/23	Friday 05/02/23	Saturday 06/02/23	Sunday 07/02/23
Key Dates							
Content Pillar							
Blog							
Email							
Instagram Grid							
Instagram Reels							
Instagram Stories							
Facebook							
TikTok							
Twitter							
Pinterest							
LinkedIn							

Here's an example of what that looks like in practice:

	Monday 01/02/23	Tuesday 02/02/23	Wednesday 03/02/23	Thursday 04/02/23	Friday 05/02/23	Saturday 06/02/23	Sunday 07/02/23
Key Dates		Launch					
Content Pillar		Our Brands		How You Wear It			Meet the Designer
Blog				Influencers wearing different pieces of the collection, plus write ups of their thoughts of the collection			Interview: Introducing Astrid Williams. Include short video of rapid-fire questions
Email		Collection launch		Influencers styling different pieces from the collection. Link to blog post			Quotes from the Astrid Williams interview. Link to blog post
Instagram Grid		Carousel post: images of collection		Carousel post: influencers styling different pieces			
Instagram Reels	'Coming soon' teaser						Edited cut of rapid-fire questions
Instagram Stories	Tease launch with question sticker for followers to guess	Series of images of collection		Additional shots of influencers wearing pieces of the collection			Series of quotes, images, and videos from the interview
Facebook	'Coming soon' teaser video	Images of collection with link to Astrid Williams page on website		Images of influencers styling different pieces from the collection			Edited cut of the Astrid Williams rapid-fire questions
TikTok				Videos of influencers styling different pieces from the collection			Edited cut of the Astrid Williams rapid fire questions

For the purpose of this, I'm imagining a calendar for an online fashion retailer that is launching a new designer brand on its website during this week. Again, dates are fictionalised, as is the name of the designer: Astrid Williams.

You could also include 'go live' times on your calendar for things like email sends, or posting on your social accounts, so you align across your channels and every team member is aware of what's happening when. This won't be necessary for all your activity but could be useful for big launches like the one I've made up above.

Note: you'll notice that not all days are filled in, which is purposeful. It works for some brands to pump out new content every day but it's not always necessary. From my experience, pushing out content 3-4 days a week gets results, if done strategically. You also don't need to be using every channel every day. **Try a few things out and test what works** - you can always adapt.

Use your other time to review what's working and what isn't, make plans, look at what else your audience is engaging with, and build relationships with customers or influencers.

It's up to you how far in advance you create your calendar. I've worked at big global brands where plans are done three or even six months in advance, and small brands where plans are done a week in advance. I'd suggest creating a skeleton plan per quarter and mapping out the 'big' moments each month so if you want to do a big campaign that involves a bit more leg work, you've got plenty of time to get it done.

Remember that production of some (not all) content can take a while, especially if you're engaging influencers or content creators who may have other work commitments. Also factor in time to write your briefs, approve the content and make any amends if necessary, and get all your ducks in a row before going live. Once you've got your bigger projects in place, you can be a bit more flexible with how far in advance you plan your other day to day content.

As I mentioned earlier in the chapter, there will be times when you want or need to deviate from your plan. Don't worry if you need to do that, it's normal and happens to every brand. If you've already created your content, don't let it go to waste. File it away and revisit it at a later date - your future self will thank you.

Chapter 9

Is Your Content Successful?

I mentioned earlier on in this book that there's a tendency to create, create, create, with the hope that 'the more the merrier'. But more doesn't always equal better, and it doesn't always equal results. That's why it's really important to measure what you've done.

Consistently reviewing your content output and the results it has driven is the best way to make sure your time and money is going to good use. It gives you a better understanding of what your audience resonates with, and gives you a clearer idea of what to focus on in future.

When it comes to content, every brand will define success differently - and that all goes back to what I mentioned in chapter 3 about the purpose of your content. **Why are you creating it and what are you hoping to achieve?**

If your focus is to grow your email database, measure how many leads you've generated through your content. If that answer is "not very many", take a look at your activity and see why that is - perhaps you need to create some more gated content, or give your audience an incentive to sign up, such as a welcome discount code or early access to promotions and sales.

If your focus is to improve engagement on your Instagram account, review which posts perform the best and look for a common thread. Is there a certain style of imagery that your followers love? A particular video format? Or engaging captions that encourage your audience to leave comments?

If your focus is to increase organic traffic, take a look at what blog posts are ranking in Google, or getting lots of backlinks. If you're not seeing much traffic to your blog, you might need to look at your SEO and rethink what keywords and topics you're targeting.

Content reports

In my previous in-house roles and for some of my clients now as a freelancer, I create monthly content reports. These reports give a top-level overview of what content was published and on what channels, with a breakdown of the results you're measuring and summaries of what 'worked' and what didn't do so well (plus my thoughts on why).

It takes a bit of work each month but it's so useful to look back on what you've done and helps you draw conclusions from your content activity, plus it helps you put actions in place. You can look back on your reports every quarter or end of year and have all your results summarised in one place, sparking inspiration and future plans.

What to measure

Blog Posts

- **Page views** and **unique page views**
- **Backlinks** (how many people are linking to your blog post in their own content?)

- Bounce rate (how many people have read your blog post but not visited any other page on your site? A high bounce rate is relatively normal for blog posts but if you're selling a product or service, ideally you want to be sending your readers to other parts of your site too)
- Traffic source (where have your readers come from? A social link? An email newsletter inclusion? Or is your SEO strong and you're getting lots of organic traffic?)

You can find this data in Google Analytics once you've hooked your site up to it, and SEO tools like SEMrush.

Instagram

- Followers (note: these will fluctuate, which is perfectly normal. You may also find you have periods of high growth and periods where your follower count doesn't really budge. Again - totally normal. But if you feel as though you're struggling to grow, take a look back at periods where you've seen high growth and see if there was anything you did differently that you could try again)
- Engagement rate per post. You can work this out with this formula: Engagement rate = (interactions / audience) x 100. According to Hootsuite, the global average Instagram engagement rates for business accounts as of October 2022 was 0.54% so if you're hitting that or higher, you're doing well
- Likes, comments, saves and shares. Are there certain posts that get more comments or saves than most? What's being shared? This will give an insight into what is resonating with your audience

You can find this data straight in the Instagram app. Make sure you have a business account on Instagram, so you get access to your 'professional dashboard'. This is a useful tool to use as it breaks down your follower demographics, engagement, and reach.

TikTok

- **Followers** (how many followers do you have? And where have you seen growth?)
- **Views** (how many people viewed your video?)
- **Likes** (how many people liked it?)
- **Comments** (how many comments did you get? And what was your audience saying?)
- **Shares** (how many people have shared your video?)

As with Instagram, make sure you have a business account on TikTok. This enables you to access your analytics. You do this by going to your profile and opening the 'settings and privacy' tab in the top right corner. Under 'Account', choose the 'Creator Tools' tab, then select 'Analytics'.

Facebook

- **Page likes** and **followers** (how many have 'liked' or followed your page?)
- **Engagement** (likes, reactions, comments, shares)

- **Engagement rate**. You can calculate that with this formula: Engagement rate = (total number of engagements / total reach number) x 100
- **Link clicks** (if you included a link to something in your post, how many people clicked on it?)
- **Reach** (how many people saw your post?)
- **Impressions** (how many times did your post show up in someone's timeline?)

You can find this data straight in the Facebook app, Facebook Creator Studio and your 'professional dashboard' (like Instagram).

YouTube

- **Subscribers** (how many people have subscribed to your channel?)
- **Watch time**. This is the total amount of minutes viewers have spent watching your videos. YouTube pushed videos and channels with higher watch times, as its algorithm assumes it's engaging. So when people search for the topic your video is on, it's more likely to feature high up in the search results
- **Audience retention**. This shows you the percentage of viewers who watch and leave your video at every single moment of the video. Like watch time, YouTube favours videos with high audience retention. It's also useful to see where viewers drop off (i.e., when they no longer find your video useful or engaging)
- **Re-watches**. This is the number of times viewers re-watch certain parts of your video. If there are certain segments of your video that

are getting a lot of re-watches, that will help you see what topics your audience engages with most

- **Likes, comments, shares**
- **Traffic sources** (where is your audience coming from? Have they found you via the search function on YouTube, or clicked a link that was shared on Facebook, for example?)

You can find all this data in YouTube Studio, plus lots of other metrics.

Pinterest

- **Impressions** (how many times did your Pin show up on a user's screen?)
- **Total audience** (the number of unique users who saw your Pin in a given period)
- **Saves** (how many people saved your Pin to one of their boards? Note: Saves used to be called 'Repins')
- **Engagements** (the total number of times someone clicked or saved your Pin)
- **Pin clicks** (how many people clicked on your Pin?)
- **Outbound clicks** (the total number of clicks to the URL you included in your Pin)

You can find all this data in your 'Analytics' tab in your Pinterest account. Make sure you have a business Pinterest account to access this.

Email

- Number of **email subscribers**
- **Open rate** (how many of your subscribers opened your email? If certain emails get more opens than most, take a deeper look at why that is. Are there subject lines that are more engaging? Are there particular days or times of day that are better to send your emails on?)
- **Click-through rate** (how many people clicked on the links in your email? Note: this will likely be much lower than your open rate)
- **Conversion rate** (how many people clicked on your link and then completed a specific action, like signing up to a webinar you're promoting or buying something you're selling?)
- **Bounce rate** (how many of your subscribers didn't receive your email? If you have a high bounce rate, chances are there are a lot of email addresses in your database that are old or fake. You can get around this by asking your subscribers to verify their email address when they sign up)
- Number of **unsubscribes** (how many people are unsubscribing from your emails? Are there certain times of year or certain emails that trigger this more than most?)

You can find all this data in whichever platform you use to build and send emails - like Klaviyo or MailChimp, for example. When choosing a platform, do your research first to see which one will work best for what you want to use it for.

Chapter 10

Get Creating

Now go, create. Try, test, adapt, and try and test again.

Some content you create won't be great. Some will flop. Some will surprise you in the reception it gets from your audience. It's all part of the fun.

I hope this book helps you on your journey to make content work for your brand. If you're ever stuck or want to pick my brain, you can find me at **angharadjones.co.uk** or **@angharadbjones** on Instagram.

About The Author

Angharad Jones is a freelance copywriter and content specialist from Wirral, England. She's spent a decade working in journalism, content marketing, and copywriting - as well as living and working in London, Manchester, Melbourne, Sydney, and Leeds.

When she's not writing or strategising for other brands or magazines, Angharad spends her time creating content for her own Instagram, perfecting her downward dog, and dreaming of her next escape.

Printed in Great Britain
by Amazon

25406174R00030